Neil Diamond
12 Greatest Hits
Vol. II

Art Direction and Design by DAVID KIRSCHNER

Yesterday's Songs

Moderately

Words and Music by NEIL DIAMOND

F(add9) F/C F F/C Am Am/E
Ba - by, yes - ter - day's blues may be yes - ter - day's news, but the
May - be yes - ter - day's rhyme was for yes - ter - day's time, and the
B♭ B♭m F F/C
truth al - ways stays the same. And the good things will nev - er change,
fu - ture's not ours to see. But there's some things that al - ways will be,
Gm7sus C7 F(add9) F/C 1 F(add9) F/C F(add9) F/C
like say - ing, "I love you," just say - ing, "I love you."
like say - ing, "I love you,"
F(add9) F/C 2 F(add9) F/C F F(add9)
like say - ing, "I love you."

September Morn

Words and Music by NEIL DIAMOND
and GILBERT BECAUD

Moderately slow

Abm7
Db9
Gbmaj7
Cbmaj7
Stay with me a while.
I on - ly wan - na talk to you.
Abm
Adim
Bb7sus
Bb7
We've trav - eled half way 'round the world __ to find our - selves __ a - gain.
Sep - tem - ber
3
Eb(add9)
Eb
Bbm7
Eb9
morn.
We danced un - til the night be - came a brand - new
mf
Ab(add9)
Ab
Abm9
Db9-5
day.
Two lov - ers play - ing scenes __ from some ro - man - tic play.

Eb(add9) Eb C11 Cm7 Fm7 Bb11
Sep - tem - ber morn-ing still can make me feel that
Eb Cm7 Fm7 Bb9
way. Look at what you've done.
dim.
mp
Ebmaj9 Cm7 Fm7 Bb9
Why, you've be-come a grown-up girl. I still can hear you cry-ing in the
Eb Fm7 F#dim Eb/G Abm7 Db9
cor - ner of your room. And look how far we've come: so

Gbmaj7
Cbmaj7
Abm
Adim
far from where we used to be, but not so far that we've for-got-ten
Bb7sus
Bb7
Eb(add9)
Eb
3
how it was__ be-fore. Sep-tem-ber morn. Do you re-
mf
Bbm7
Eb9
Ab(add9)
Ab
mem-ber__ how we danced__ that night a-way? Two lov-ers
Abm9
Db9-5
Eb
Cm7
play-ing scenes__ from some ro-man-tic play. Sep-tem-ber

Fm7 Ab/Bb Bb9 Eb Fm7 F#dim Eb/G
morn-ing still can make me feel that way.
Abm7 Db9 Gbmaj7 Cbmaj7 Abm Adim
Fm7/Bb C13 F(add9) F
Sep - tem - ber morn. We
f
Cm7 F9 Bb(add9) Bb
danced un - til the night be - came a brand new day. Two lov - ers

Bbm9
Eb9-5
F
Dm7
play - ing scenes from some ro - man - tic play.
Sep - tem - ber
Gm7
Gm7/C
F
Gm7/C
morn-ing still can make me feel that way.
Sep - tem - ber
3
F(add9)
F
Cm7/F
F9
morn.
We danced un - til the night be - came a brand - new
Bb(add9)
Bb
Eb11
Eb9-5
day.
Two lov - ers
play - ing scenes from some ro - man - tic play.

F/C
Dm7
Gm7
Gm7/C
Sep - tem - ber morn-ing still can make me feel that
dim.
F
Dm7
Gm7
Gm7/C
F
Dm7
way.
Sep- tem- ber
mf
Gm7
Gm7/C
F
Eb/Bb
morn-ing still can make me feel that way.
dim.
mp
Db/Ab
Gm7-5
C11
F(add9)
rit.

Love On The Rocks

Words and Music by NEIL DIAMOND
and GILBERT BECAUD

Moderately slow Ballad

F
B7
Got noth - in' to lose, so you just sing the blues all the
E
Am
time. Gave you my heart,
F
G
gave you my soul. You left me a - lone here with
Em7
F
B7
noth-ing to hold. Yes - ter - day's gone. Now all I want is a

E
E/D
A/C#
E/B
A
smile.
First they say they want you,
mf
Amaj7
G/A
how they real-ly need you.
Sud-den-ly, you find you're out there,
D/A
F
G
A
walk-ing in a storm.
When they know they have you,
Amaj7
A7
D6/A
Dm6/A
then they real-ly have you.
Noth-ing you can do or say.
You've

A
G9
E
To Coda
got to leave, just get a - way.
We all know the song.
Am
C/G
F
You need what you need,
you can say what you want.
mp
G
G/F
Em7
Not much you can do when the feel - ing is gone.
May - be
F
B7
blue skies a - bove,
but it's cold
when your love's on the

D.S. al Coda
CODA
E
E/D A/C# E/B
Am
rocks.
Love on the rocks
mp
F
G
ain't no sur - prise.
Pour me a drink,
and I'll
Em7
F
tell you some lies.
Yes - ter - day's gone,
B7
E
Am
3
and now all I want is a smile.
rit.
p

You Don't Bring Me Flowers

Words by NEIL DIAMOND, MARILYN BERGMAN
and ALAN BERGMAN
Music by NEIL DIAMOND

Slowly and freely

C G/C F/C C
you could-n't wait to love me, used to hate to leave me.
a tempo
Fmaj7 G7sus G7
Now af - ter lov - in' me late at night when it's
gradual cresc.
C Fmaj7 G7sus G7
good for you and you're feel - in' all right, well, you
C Em7 Am7 Ab Bb/Ab
just roll o - ver, and you turn out the light.
f
decresc.
molto rit.
mp

C/G
G7sus
G7
C
G/C
And you don't bring me flow - ers an - y - more.
a tempo
F/C
G11
C
G/C
It used to be so nat - 'ral
F/C
C
F
C/E
to talk a-bout for - ev - er, but used-to-be's don't count an - y - more. They just
Dm7
Fmaj7
G7
C
G/C
lay on the floor till we sweep them a-way. And ba - by, I re - mem - ber
gradual cresc.

F/C
C
Fmaj7
all the things you taught me: I learned how to laugh, and I
G7sus
G7
C
Fmaj7
learned how to cry. Well, I learned how to love, e - ven
G7sus
G7
C
Em7
learned how to lie. You'd think I could learn how to
Am7
Ab
Bb/Ab
C/G
G7sus
G7
tell you good - bye, 'cause you don't bring me flow - ers an - y -

Am
D7sus
D7
more.
a tempo
decresc.
C/G
C6/G
G7sus
G7
Well, you'd
mp
cresc.
ff
C
Em7
Am
Ab
Bb/Ab
think I could learn how to tell you good - bye,
rit.
decresc.
C/G
G7sus
G7
C
Cmaj7
C6
C/G
C
'cause you don't bring me flow - ers an - y - more.
mp
a tempo
rit.

Desirée

Moderate Rock beat

Words and Music by NEIL DIAMOND

F/C C F/C C
on that young - er day. Well, I be -
on that sleep - less night. Well, I
came a man at the hands of a girl al - most twice
tossed and I turned while the thought of her burned up and down
G C
my age. And she came to me
my mind. For she was there and gone
F/C C F/C C
just like a morn - ing sun, and it was -
with - out one re - gret, but she con -

G
n't so much_ her words__ as such__ as the way they were sung.__
tin - ues__ on__ like the words of a song I could not for - get.__
C
Am
G/B
It was the way they were sung.__
I could not for - get.
De -
C
C6
si - rée, oh De - si - rée, there I was found by the sweet_
Cmaj7
C
F
G
__ pas - sion sound of your lov - ing song.
Time was right, the

G7 G7/A G7/B C
night was long. Re-mem-ber, De - si-rée, oh De-
C6 Cmaj7 C F
- si-rée. Some-how, I knew I could on-ly have you till the
G
morn-ing light. If on-ly for that sin-gle night,
The night was long, the time was right.
1 G7 C F/C C
sweet De-si-rée, you made it right.

Am
Then came the
2
G7
G7/A
G7/B
Repeat and Fade
C
Do you re-mem-ber, De - si-rée, oh De - si-rée?
C6
Cmaj7
C
F
G
G7
G7/A
G7/B
Do you re-mem-ber, De -

America

Moderately bright

Words and Music by NEIL DIAMOND

but not with - out a star.
Free, on - ly want to be free.
We hud - dle close,
hang on to a dream.

G
On the boats and on the planes,
they're com - ing to A -
mer - i - ca.
Nev - er look - ing back a - gain,
D/F#
Em
they're com - ing to A - mer - i - ca.
Home,
D
G
C/E
G
don't it seem so far a-way.
Oh, we're trav - el - ing

D
Em
F
light to - day,
in the eye of the storm,
G/D
F/Eb
Em
in the eye of the storm.
3
D
G
Home
to a new and a shin - y place.
C/E
G
D
Em
Make our bed, and we'll say our grace.
Free - dom's light burn - ing

F
G/D
F/E♭
Em
warm,
free - dom's light burn - ing
warm.
F
Ev - 'ry - where a - round
the world,
they're com - ing to A - mer - i - ca.

Ev - 'ry time that flag's un - furled, they're com - ing to A - mer - i - ca.
G
Got a dream to take them there.
They're com - ing to A - mer - i - ca.
Got a dream, they've come to share.
They're com - ing to A - mer - i - ca.

A
F#m7
They're com - ing to A - mer - i - ca. They're com - ing to A -
D
mer - i - ca. They're com - ing to A - mer - i - ca.
Bm7
A
They're com - ing to A - mer - i - ca to - day,
F#m7
D
to - day,
to - day,

Bm7
A
to - day,
to - day.
My
F#m
coun - try 'tis of thee (to - day),
sweet land of lib - er - ty (to - day
D
Bm
), of thee I sing (to - day), of thee I sing to - day.
F
Repeat and fade
To - day,
to - day.

America

Words and Music by NEIL DIAMOND

▼

Far, we've been traveling far
Without a home
But not without a star

Free, only want to be free
We huddle close
Hang onto a dream

On the boats and on the planes
They're coming to America
Never looking back again
They're coming to America

Home, don't it seem so far away
Oh, we're traveling light today
In the eye of the storm
In the eye of the storm

Home, to a new and a shiny place
Make our bed, and we'll say our grace
Freedom's light burning warm
Freedom's light burning warm

Everywhere around the world
They're coming to America
Every time that flag's unfurled
They're coming to America

Got a dream to take them there
They're coming to America
Got a dream they've come to share
They're coming to America

They're coming to America
They're coming to America
They're coming to America
They're coming to America
Today

▲

Be

Words and Music by NEIL DIAMOND

▼

Lost on a painted sky
Where the clouds are hung
For the poet's eye
You may find him
If you may find him

There on a distant shore
By the wings of dreams
Through an open door
You may know him
If you may

Be, as a page that aches for a word
Which speaks on a theme that is timeless
While the Sun God will make for your day
Sing, as a song in search of a voice
That is silent
And the one God will make
For your way

We dance
To a whispered voice
Overheard by the soul
Undertook by the heart
And you may know it
If you may know it

While the sand
Would become the stone
Which begat the spark
Turned to living bone
Holy, holy
Sanctus, Sanctus

▲

Beautiful Noise

Words and Music by NEIL DIAMOND

▼

What a beautiful noise
Comin' up from the street
Got a beautiful sound
It's got a beautiful beat

It's a beautiful noise
Goin' on everywhere
Like the clickety clack
Of a train on a track
It's got rhythm to spare

It's a beautiful noise
And it's a sound that I love
And it fits me as well
As a hand in a glove
Yes it does, yes it does

What a beautiful noise
Comin' up from the park
It's the song of the kids
And it plays until dark

It's the song of the cars
On their furious flights
But there's even romance
In the way that they dance
To the beat of the lights

It's a beautiful noise
And it's a sound that I love
And it makes me feel good
Like a hand in a glove
Yes it does, yes it does
What a beautiful noise

It's a beautiful noise
Made of joy and of strife
Like a symphony played
By the passing parade
It's the music of life

What a beautiful noise
Comin' into my room
And it's beggin' for me
Just to give it a tune

▲

Desirée

Words and Music by NEIL DIAMOND

▼

It was the third of June
On that younger day
Well, I became a man
At the hands of a girl
Almost twice my age
And she came to me
Just like a morning sun
And it wasn't so much
Her words as such
As the way they were sung
It was the way they were sung

Desirée
Oh, Desirée
There I was found
By the sweet passion sound
Of your loving song
Time was right, the night was long
Remember, Desirée
Oh, Desirée
Somehow I knew
I could only have you
'Til the morning light
If only for that single night
Sweet Desirée, you made it right

Then came the fourth of June
On that sleepless night
Well, I tossed and I turned
While the thought of her burned
Up and down my mind
For, she was there and gone
Without one regret
But, she continues on
Like the words of a song
I could not forget
I could not forget

Desirée
Oh, Desirée
There I was found
By the sweet passion sound
Of your loving song
Time was right, the night was long
Remember, Desirée
Oh, Desirée
And though somehow I knew
I could only have you
'Til the morning light
The night was long, the time was right
Do you remember, Desirée

▲

Forever In Blue Jeans

Words and Music by NEIL DIAMOND and RICHARD BENNETT

▼

Money talks
But it don't sing and dance
And it don't walk
And long as I
Can have you here with me
I'd much rather be
Forever in blue jeans

Honey's sweet
But it ain't nothing next to
Baby's treat
And if you pardon me
I'd like to say
We'll do okay
Forever in blue jeans

Maybe tonight
Maybe tonight, you and I
All alone by the fire
Nothing around
But the sound of my heart
And your sighs

Money talks
But it can't sing and dance
And it can't walk
And long as I
Can have you here with me
I'd much rather be
Forever in blue jeans, babe

▲

Hello Again

Words by NEIL DIAMOND
Music by NEIL DIAMOND and ALAN LINDGREN

▼

Hello again, hello
Just called to say 'hello'
I couldn't sleep at all tonight
And I know it's late
But I couldn't wait

Hello, my friend, hello
Just called to let you know
I think about you every night
When I'm here alone
And you're there at home
Hello

Maybe it's been crazy
And maybe I'm to blame
But I put my heart above my head
We've been through it all
And you loved me just the same
And when you're not there
I just need to hear

Hello, my friend, hello
It's good to need you so
It's good to love you like I do
And to feel this way
When I hear you say
Hello

Hello, my friend, hello
Just called to let you know
I think about you every night
And I know it's late
But I couldn't wait
Hello

▲

If You Know What I Mean

Words and Music by NEIL DIAMOND

▼

When the night returns just like a friend
When the evening comes to set me free
When the quiet hours that wait beyond the day
Make peaceful sounds in me

Took a drag from my last cigarette
Took a drink from a glass of old wine
I closed my eyes, and I could make it real
And feel it one more time

Can you hear it, babe
Can you hear it, babe
From another time
From another place
Do you remember it, babe

And the radio played
Like a carnival tune
As we lay in our bed
In the other room

When we gave it away
For the sake of a dream
In a penny arcade
If you know what I mean

Here's to the songs we used to sing
And here's to the times we used to know
It's hard to hold them in our arms again
And hard to let them go

Do you hear it, babe
Do you hear it, babe
It was another time
It was another place
Do you remember it, babe

▲

Longfellow Serenade

Words and Music by NEIL DIAMOND

▼

Longfellow Serenade
Such were the plans I'd made
For she was a lady
And I was a dreamer
With only words to trade

You know that I was born for a night like this
Warmed by a stolen kiss
For I was lonely
And she was lonely

Ride, come on, baby, ride
Let me make your dreams come true
I'll sing my song
Let me sing my song
Let me make it warm for you

I'll weave his web of rhyme
Upon the summer night
We'll leave this worldly time
On his winged flight

Then come, and as we lay
Beside this sleepy glade
There I will sing to you
My Longfellow Serenade

Longfellow Serenade
Such were the plans I made
But she was a lady
As deep as the river
And through the night, we stayed

And, in my way, I loved her as none before
Loved her with words and more
For she was lonely
And I was lonely

▲

Love On The Rocks

Words and Music by NEIL DIAMOND and GILBERT BECAUD

▼

Love on the rocks
Ain't no surprise
Pour me a drink
And I'll tell you some lies
Got nothin' to lose
So you just sing the blues all the time

Gave you my heart
Gave you my soul
You left me alone here
With nothing to hold
Yesterday's gone
Now all I want is a smile

First, they say they want you
How they really need you
Suddenly, you find you're out there
Walking in a storm
When they know they have you
Then, they really have you
Nothing you can do or say
You've got to leave, just get away
We all know the song

You need what you need
You can say what you want
Not much you can do
When the feeling is gone
May be blue skies above
But it's cold
When your love's on the rocks

First, they say they want you
How they really need you
Suddenly, you find you're out there
Walking in a storm
When they know they have you
Then, they really have you
Nothing you can do or say
You've got to leave, just get away
We all know the song

Love on the rocks
Ain't no surprise
Pour me a drink
And I'll tell you some lies
Yesterday's gone
And now all I want is a smile

▲

September Morn

Words and Music by NEIL DIAMOND and GILBERT BECAUD

▼

Stay for just a while
Stay, and let me look at you
It's been so long, I hardly knew you
Standing in the door
Stay with me a while
I only wanna talk to you
We've traveled halfway 'round the world
To find ourselves again

September morn
We danced until the night became a brand new day
Two lovers playing scenes from some romantic play
September morning still can make me feel that way

Look at what you've done
Why, you've become a grown-up girl
I still can hear you crying
In the corner of your room
And look how far we've come
So far from where we used to be
But not so far that we've forgotten
How it was before

September morn
Do you remember how we danced that night away
Two lovers playing scenes from some romantic play
September morning still can make me feel that way

▲

Yesterday's Songs

Words and Music by NEIL DIAMOND

▼

Yesterday's songs
Don't stay around long
Not much anymore

Yesterday's words
Don't make themselves heard
Like they did before

Baby, yesterday's blues
May be yesterday's news
But the truth always stays the same
And the good things will never change
Like sayin', "I love you"
Sayin', "I love you"

Yesterday's songs
Don't seem to belong
They're here, and they're gone

Yesterday's moves
Don't stay in the grooves
They keep moving on

Maybe yesterday's rhyme
Was for yesterday's time
And the future's not ours to see
But there's some things that always will be
Like sayin', "I love you"
Sayin', "I love you"

▲

You Don't Bring Me Flowers

Words by NEIL DIAMOND, MARILYN BERGMAN and ALAN BERGMAN
Music by NEIL DIAMOND

▼

You don't bring me flowers
You don't sing me love songs
You hardly talk to me anymore
When you come through the door
At the end of the day

I remember when
You couldn't wait to love me
Used to hate to leave me
Now, after lovin' me late at night
When it's good for you
And you're feelin' all right
Well, you just roll over
And you turn out the light
And you don't bring me flowers anymore

It used to be so natural
To talk about forever
But used to be's don't count anymore
They just lay on the floor
'Til we sweep them away

And baby, I remember
All the things you taught me
I learned how to laugh
And I learned how to cry
Well, I learned how to love
Even learned how to lie
You'd think I could learn
How to tell you goodbye
'Cause you don't bring me flowers anymore

▲

Hello Again

Words by NEIL DIAMOND
Music by NEIL DIAMOND
and ALAN LINDGREN

Moderately slow

Fmaj7/G G7 F/G G7 C(add9) G7sus C(add9) G7sus
could - n't wait. Hel - lo, my friend, hel - lo. Just
C(add9) G7sus C(add9) Em7/B Am F Dm7
called to let you know I think a - bout you
Em7 Am7 G7sus
ev - 'ry night when I'm here a - lone and you're
Fmaj7/G G7 F/G G7 C(add9)
there at home. Hel - lo.

F Em7 F G C
May - be it's been cra - zy, and may - be I'm to blame,
F Em7 Dm7 G7sus G/F
but I put my heart a - bove my head.
Em7 Am Em7 Am
We've been through it all, and you loved me just the same.
Em7 Am Dm7/G G7
3
And when you're not there, I just need to hear: Hel -

C(add9) G7sus C(add9) G7sus C(add9) G7sus
lo, my friend, hel - lo. It's good to need you
C(add9) Em7/B Am F Dm7 Em7 Am7
so. It's good to love you like I do and to
G7sus G7 F/G C
feel this way when I hear you say 'hel - lo'.
F Dm7 Em7 Am7 G7sus Ab7
Hel -

Db(add 9) Ab7sus Db(add 9) Ab7sus Db(add 9) Ab7sus
lo, my friend, hel - lo, Just called to let you
f
Db(add 9) Fm7/C Bbm Gb Ebm7 Fm7 Bbm7
know I think a - bout you ev - 'ry night. And I
Ab11 Ab7 Ab11 Ab7
know it's late, but I could - n't wait. Hel -
Db(add 9) Ebm7/Bb Db/Ab Ab7sus Ab7 Db
lo.
mp
rit.

Forever In Blue Jeans

Words and Music by NEIL DIAMOND
and RICHARD BENNETT

Moderately

D
A
Bm
it don't walk.
And long as I can have you here with me, I'd
C#m
E
A
E
D/F#
C/G
E/G#
much rath-er be for-ev-er in blue jeans.
A
D
Hon-ey's sweet.
But it ain't noth-ing next to ba-by's treat.
A
Bm
C#m
E
And if you par-don me, I'd like to say we'll do o-kay for-ev-er in

A
A
blue jeans.
May - be to - night.
cresc.
sub. p
A7
D/A
Dm/A
A
May - be to - night, you and I all a - lone by the fire;
G
D
Dsus
noth - ing a - round but the sound of my heart
E
and your sighs.
cresc.

walkdown E D D♭ B
walk up E F# G A♭
G→A
open A
A
Mon - ey talks. But it can't sing and dance and
mf
D
it can't walk. And long as I can have you here with me, I'd
A
Bm
C#m
E
To Coda
A
much rath - er be for - ev - er in blue jeans, babe.
E
D/F#
C/G
E/G#
A
Hon - ey's sweet. But it ain't noth - ing next to

D A Bm
ba-by's treat. And if you par-don me, I'd like to say we'll
C#m E A
D.S. al Coda
do o-kay for-ev-er in blue jeans.
cresc.
CODA
A D
blue jeans, babe.
blue jeans, babe.
A Bm C#m E
Repeat and Fade
And if you par-don me, I'd like to say we'll do o-kay for-ev-er in
And long as I can have you here with me, I'd much rath-er be for-ev-er in

Longfellow Serenade

Bright Rock tempo

Words and Music by NEIL DIAMOND

E
she was a la - dy, and I was a dream - er with on - ly words to trade.
she was a la - dy as deep as the ri - ver, and through the night we stayed.
A
You know that I was born for a night like this,
And in my way, I loved her as none be - fore,
A
E
warmed by a sto - len kiss.
For I was lone - ly,
loved her with words and more.
For she was lone - ly,
B7
and she was lone - ly.
and I was lone - ly.

E
Emaj7
E7
Ride, come on ba - by, ride. Let me make your dreams
A
E
B7
come true. I'll sing my
E
Emaj7
song; let me sing my song.
E7
A
E
Let me make it warm for

B7
E
you.
I'll weave his web of rhyme
A
upon the summer night.
We'll
B7
leave this worldly time
on his winged flight.
E
Then come, and as we lay

A
be - side this sleep - y glade,
there I will sing
E
B7
E
To Coda
to you my Long - fel - low Se - re - nade.
D
A/C♯
E/B
A
E(add9)
D.S. al Coda
ped.
D
A/C♯
E/B
A
E
CODA
E
Fine

Be

from JONATHAN LIVINGSTON SEAGULL, the film by Hall Bartlett

Words and Music by NEIL DIAMOND

G/D
D
dis - tant shore __ by the wings of dreams __ through an o - pen door, __
G
A
you may know him, __ if you may. __
8va continues
A7
D
Be as a page that aches _ for a
mf
loco
G
D
word which speaks _ on a theme that is time - less __ while the

G
D
3
3
sun god will make for your day.
3
3
D
G
D
Sing as a song in search of a voice that is si - lent,
G
D
3
and the one God will make for your way.
3

1
2
D
G/D
D
mp
And we dance to a whis-pered voice, ov-er-
G/D
D
G/D
8va
D
G
heard by the soul, un-der-took by the heart, and you may know it,
8va continues
D
if you may know it. While the sand would be-

G/D
D
G/D
D
G/D
D
come the stone, which be - gat the spark, turned to liv - ing bone.
loco
G
A
A7
D.S. al Coda
Ho - ly, Ho - ly. Sanc - tus, Sanc - tus.
CODA
rit.

If You Know What I Mean

Words and Music by NEIL DIAMOND

Introduction

Bm Dmaj7/A G D/F♯ G Em7 A A6 A7
yond the day make peace - ful sounds in me.
D A/C♯ D
Took a drag from my last ci - ga - rette,
mp
G A7 D D/F♯ G A7
took a drink from a glass of old wine.
I closed my eyes, and I could
Bm Dmaj7/A G D/F♯ G Em7 A7
make it real and feel it one more time.
Can you
p

Bm
hear it babe?
hear it babe?
cresc. poco a poco
A
Can you hear it babe?
Do you hear it babe?
G
D/F♯
Em
D
D/F♯
Em
D
From an - oth - er time, from an - oth - er place, do you re -
It was an - oth - er time, it was an - oth - er place. Do you re -
f
A
D/A
A7
D
mem - ber it babe?
mem - ber it babe?
And the ra - di - o played like a car - ni - val
ff
Em7
D/F♯
tune as we lay in our bed in the o - ther room, when we gave it a - way for the sake of a
3

G G/A To Coda D
dream in a pen - ny ar - cade, if you know what I mean.
mp ff
F Em D G/D D G/D D A/C#
Here's to the songs we used to
dim. mp
D D/F# G A7
sing, and here's to the times we used to know.
D D/F# G A7
It's hard to hold them in our
cresc.

Bm Dmaj7/A G D/F# G Em7 A
D.S. al Coda
arms a - gain and hard to let them go. Do you
CODA
D G
mean. If you know what I
D G D
mean. If you know what I mean.
f
G D F Em D
If you know what I mean.
ff
molto rit.

Beautiful Noise

Moderately

Words and Music by NEIL DIAMOND

A
It's a beau-ti-ful noise
go-in' on ev-'ry-where.
A7
Like the click-e-ty clack of a train on a track, it's got rhy-thm to spare.
D
G
It's a beau-ti-ful noise;
and it's a sound that I love.
C
C7
And it fits me as

F
G C/G G
well as a hand in a glove. Yes it does;
C/G G G C/G G7 C/G G
yes it does. What a beau-ti-ful
C G
noise com-in' up from the park. It's the song of the kids,
G7 C
and it plays un-til dark. It's the song of the

C
G
cars on their fu - ri - ous flights,
noise made of joy and of strife,
G7
but there's e - ven ro - mance in the way that they dance to the beat of the lights.
like a sym - pho - ny played by the pass - ing pa - rade it's the mu - sic of life.
C
F
It's a beau - ti - ful noise,
G
and it's a sound that I love.
And it fits me as well
And it makes me feel good,

F
G C/G G
as a hand in a glove.
like a hand in a glove.
Yes it does;
G C/G G G C/G G7 C/G G
yes it does.
What a beau - ti - ful
C G
noise
com-in' in-to my room.
And it's beg - gin' for
3
G7 C
me
just to give it a tune.
rit.